BACKYARD ANIMALS
SQUIRRELS

by Kristin Petrie

Checkerboard
Library

An Imprint of Abdo Publishing
www.abdopublishing.com

www.abdopublishing.com

Published by Abdo Publishing, a division of ABDO, PO Box 398166, Minneapolis, Minnesota 55439.
Copyright © 2015 by Abdo Consulting Group, Inc. International copyrights reserved in all countries. No part of this book may be reproduced in any form without written permission from the publisher. Checkerboard Library™ is a trademark and logo of Abdo Publishing.

Printed in the United States of America, North Mankato, Minnesota.
102014
012015

Cover Photos: iStockphoto
Interior Photos: Alamy pp. 9, 17; AP Images p. 15; Glow Images p. 9; iStockphoto pp. 1, 5, 6, 11, 13, 21, 27, 29;
    Science Source pp. 12, 18, 19, 22–23; SuperStock p. 25

Series Coordinator: Megan M. Gunderson
Editors: Rochelle Baltzer, Bridget O'Brien
Art Direction: Neil Klinepier

Library of Congress Cataloging-in-Publication Data
Petrie, Kristin, 1970- author.
 Squirrels / Kristin Petrie.
    pages cm. -- (Backyard animals)
 Audience: Ages 8-12.
 Includes index.
 ISBN 978-1-62403-663-7
1. Squirrels--Juvenile literature. I. Title.
 QL737.R68P43 2015
 599.36--dc23
                      2014024643

TABLE OF CONTENTS

SQUIRRELS

Squirrels. Many people love to watch their crazy antics and acrobatics on trees, roofs, and bird feeders. To others, squirrels are destructive, unwanted pests. Squirrels like to steal bird feed, eat corn, and gnaw on tree bark.

Squirrels are found in natural and human-made **habitats** on nearly every continent. They survive on their own in forests. They also happily accept food from homeowners or from strangers in the park.

Squirrels are mammals from the scientific order Rodentia. They share this order with other rodents, such as rats, beavers, and chipmunks. Squirrels make up the family Sciuridae, which includes nearly 300 species! Some of the most common squirrel species in North American backyards are eastern gray squirrels, American red squirrels, and eastern fox squirrels.

SCIENTIFIC CLASSIFICATION

Kingdom: Animalia
Phylum: Chordata
Class: Mammalia
Order: Rodentia
Family: Sciuridae

The family Sciuridae includes tree squirrels (*below*), ground squirrels, and flying squirrels.

ORIGIN & HABITAT

Scientists believe squirrels **evolved** from their rodent cousins 30 to 40 million years ago. Today, they are found on five continents. They do not live in Australia or Antarctica.

The red squirrel's geographic range is vast. This species is found to the north throughout Alaska and Canada. Its range extends as

far south as New Mexico. And, red squirrels live along the East Coast. However, they do not live in the western or far southern United States.

Eastern gray squirrels aren't just found in the east! They live in the Midwest and the South. They are also found in Canada in

ALMOST EVERYWHERE

Squirrels are not found on Greenland, Madagascar, or many other islands.

6

Saskatchewan, Manitoba, Ontario, and Quebec. Fox squirrels have a very similar range. They just live slightly farther west. And, they do not live in the northeast.

The widespread squirrel family also occupies a wide range of **habitats**. These vary from **arid** grasslands to drenched rain forests and arctic **tundras**. And of course, they live in cities and **suburbs**!

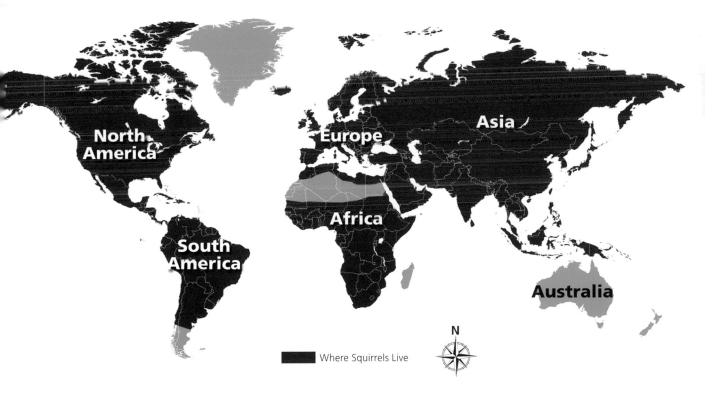

Where Squirrels Live

The squirrel is highly adaptable, so its home depends on its location. Red squirrels prefer **temperate** to polar forest regions. They like forests with tall pine trees. But, they are also found in **deciduous** forests. And, they seek out areas with mushrooms for **foraging**. Some make their homes in **urban** areas, as long as there are enough trees and food sources.

The eastern gray squirrel also prefers forested areas for its **habitat**. This species likes forests with a mix of trees such as oak, walnut, and pine. These trees produce long-lasting foods such as nuts for winter feeding. They also form a continuous forest **canopy**.

Eastern gray, fox, and red squirrels are all tree squirrels. Tree squirrels are mainly **arboreal**. They spend most of their time high up in the forest canopy. Traveling and foraging in trees protects them from some predators. A forest provides multiple escape routes from danger.

These squirrels use trees for their homes. They build nests, but they also use natural dens, such as tree holes. These places are well made and are built to be hidden. So, they are useful for protecting very young squirrels.

TREE SQUIRREL COUSINS
Ground squirrels usually make their nests underground or at ground level in fallen trees.

Eastern gray squirrels use leaves and twigs to build their nests 30 to 45 feet (9 to 14 m) up. They usually build nests where branches fork.

Red squirrels build nests 7 to 66 feet (2 to 20 m) off the ground. They use grass, moss, and bark. They also gather fur, feathers, and other materials.

LARGE EYES TO BUSHY TAIL

Squirrels range greatly in size. The African pygmy squirrel is the smallest species. It measures just 5 inches (13 cm) long from nose to tail. The Indian giant squirrel is up to 3 feet (1 m) long! Within a species, males and females are usually the same size.

Common North American species are somewhere in the middle. The red squirrel is 11 to 15 inches (27 to 39 cm) long. This includes the tail, which is 4 to 6 inches (9 to 16 cm) in length. Red squirrels weigh about 8 ounces (213 g).

Eastern gray squirrels are larger than their red cousins. These squirrels range from 15 to 21 inches (37 to 53 cm) long. Their tails add another 6 to 9 inches (15 to 23 cm) to their length. Eastern gray squirrels weigh 12 to 26 ounces (340 to 740 g). Fox squirrels are larger still! They measure 18 to 28 inches (45 to 70 cm) and weigh 28 ounces (800 g).

GLIDING HIGH

Have you ever seen a flying squirrel? It has special skin that connects its wrists and ankles to its body. This allows it to glide between treetops!

THE SQUIRREL

TAIL

EARS

EYE

NOSE

PAWS

Squirrels can use their tails as blankets in cold weather and for shade in hot weather.

All these tree squirrels have short heads with large eyes. They have four large front teeth that never stop growing. They must gnaw on things to keep these teeth short and sharp. The squirrel's long body sprouts strong legs, furry feet, and sharp claws. A long, bushy tail completes the picture. The tail helps the squirrel balance high up in the trees.

Males and females of the same species generally have similar coats. The red squirrel's coat is usually red! It can also be gray or brown. There is a red to brown band down the center of the back. And, a dark line separates the back color from the white to cream belly. Red squirrels also have a white ring around each eye. The tail is red, yellowish, or gray with a black band running its length.

Eastern gray squirrels are light to dark gray with some cinnamon coloring. The eastern gray's tail and ears are light gray to white. Its belly is gray to buff. Some eastern grays are all black. Rarely, these squirrels are all white. Fox squirrels have similar coloring. But, their bellies may be reddish-brown, cinnamon, or yellowish instead of pale gray or white.

How do squirrels climb down trees headfirst? They turn their feet around backward!

FURRY EARS
Red squirrels and fox squirrels develop extra tufts of fur on their ears in winter.

NUTS & MORE

Squirrels are omnivores, so they eat both plants and animals. The squirrel's plant diet consists mainly of leaves, seeds, grains, and nuts. Animal-based foods include eggs, birds, insects, and other animals. People food is also a welcome treat to many squirrel populations!

The red squirrel's diet is mostly seeds of pine trees. When these are not available, the squirrel eats many other foods. These include mushrooms, tree buds, sap, and bark. Red squirrels also consume fruit, flowers, insects, eggs, and even young snowshoe hares.

Eastern gray squirrels feed on nuts, seeds, flowers, fruits, and bulbs. They also consume buds from a wide range of trees, including oak, walnut, elm, hickory, pecan, beech, and maple. The eastern gray squirrel enjoys crops, as well, such as corn and wheat. Young birds, insects, frogs, and even other squirrels may be included in its diet. The fox squirrel has a similar diet of tree seeds. It will also eat moths, beetles, and even dead fish.

Squirrels **forage** for food to eat, but they also seek food to store. This is essential for winter

THIRSTY!
Squirrels get some water from the food they eat. They also drink from puddles, streams, ponds, and tree holes.

Squirrels are careful to store foods that will keep a long time, such as nuts and seeds.

months, when less is available. Food **caches** are generally in the ground or in tree hollows. Some squirrels keep lots of food in one place, called a midden.

Others do something called scatter hoarding. They put small amounts of food in numerous locations. So if another animal finds the cache, the squirrel doesn't lose all of its food. If the squirrel moves its nest, there will likely still be food stored nearby. Squirrels use their good memories and sense of smell to find caches again.

BABY SQUIRRELS

Most squirrel species reproduce once or twice per year. The number of times depends greatly on the region and climate. If the squirrels only breed once, it is usually in late winter or early spring. In warmer climates, squirrels generally breed once in the spring and once in late summer or fall.

Red squirrels living in warm climates breed between March and May. They breed a second time between August and September. Red squirrels living in colder climates breed only in spring.

Eastern gray squirrels usually breed two times per year. One breeding season occurs between December and February. A second season takes place between May and June. Fox squirrels have a similar schedule of December and June.

To mate, males chase females through the trees. The male that keeps up with the female wins the right to mate with her. After mating, the father squirrel does not provide any help to the mother squirrel. She is responsible for raising her young.

Males chase females through the trees before mating. They use calls to communicate during this time.

HOW MANY BABIES?

If there is lots of food available, a squirrel may have more babies at one time. Usually, the second litter in a year is smaller.

If necessary, a mother squirrel will carry her young to a new nest.

Female squirrels are **pregnant** for anywhere from 25 to 65 days depending on their species and their size. A red squirrel is pregnant for about 35 days and has one to eight babies. The babies weigh just 0.2 ounces (7 g). Fox and eastern gray squirrels are pregnant for about 44 days.

EXTRA TALENTS

Flying squirrels stay with their mother for longer than some other species. This may be because they need to learn an extra skill, gliding!

Fox squirrels have up to seven babies, but average two to three. Eastern grays usually have two to four babies.

Baby squirrels are born in a nest or a tree hole. They stay there for some time, because they are born with their eyes and ears sealed shut. They completely depend on their mother for care. An eastern gray mother can be very territorial and **aggressive** around her nest when she has babies to protect.

Eastern gray squirrels are born mostly hairless. They have a few whisker-like hairs that are used for touch.

Baby squirrels continue growing in the nest. The eyes and ears open, and they begin to grow fur. Soon, they start exploring outside the nest. Young squirrels drink their mother's milk for 10 to 12 weeks. After this, they learn to become independent.

Squirrels can live 8 to 14 years in the wild. Females usually live longer than males. However, most squirrels do not survive their first year.

BUSY DAYS

Young squirrels leave their nest to find their own territory. A squirrel's home range size depends on its species and **habitat**. For example, a red squirrel's territory ranges from two to six acres (1 to 2.4 ha) in size. Male fox squirrels have larger territories than females. If there are a lot of eastern gray squirrels in one area, their home ranges will be smaller.

Sometimes, eastern fox squirrels share a nest in winter. But females do not share when they are raising young. This species is not very social.

Red squirrels will defend their territories **aggressively**! This is especially true of those that live in pine forests. They compete for pinecones to store for winter. Red squirrels that live in **deciduous** forests are less territorial. Instead of defending a large home range, they may focus more on nests and food **caches**.

The squirrel's territorial behavior extends to its mating behavior. Males interact aggressively for dominance over other males. Those with dominance generally have first pick of female squirrels for mating.

Even in winter, red squirrels rarely go more than one day without leaving the nest to search for food.

UP ALL NIGHT
Flying squirrels are nocturnal.

Tree squirrels are diurnal. This means they are active mainly during the day. Eastern gray squirrels are most active during the two hours after sunrise and the two to five hours before sunset. This helps them rest during the hottest part of the day in summer.

During cold winter months, tree squirrels do not **hibernate**. Their peak activity and **foraging** simply reduces to one time per day. Squirrels venture out in the hours before sunset because this is the warmest time of day.

Red squirrels are sometimes active at night. But usually, they are active during the morning and afternoon in warmer months. In fall, they stay active all day. This helps them prepare for winter. On the coldest days, red squirrels become less active and may not leave the nest.

ASLEEP ALL WINTER
Some ground squirrel species hibernate in winter.

SENSES & SOUNDS

Squirrels use many forms of communication. For example, red squirrels are especially known for their calls. These include growling, buzzing, chirping, and rattling. Calls are warnings to trespassers. They are used to chase away males during mating. And, they can frighten off predators.

Squirrels also have strong senses of smell, hearing, and sight. Their sense of smell assists them while **foraging** and finding their stored food.

Some squirrels practice scent marking. This sends messages to other squirrels that predators may not notice. They leave their scent on things rather than making sounds to communicate, which could give away their location. A strong sense of hearing helps in detecting predators, too.

The sense of sight is also important, because squirrels communicate with signals. An eastern gray squirrel will flick its tail to send a message. A fox squirrel will stand up, put its tail over its back, and flick it to threaten another squirrel.

Squirrels use sounds to communicate with each other and with other animals. They also move their ears, eyes, tails, and feet to express themselves.

LIKE A CAT

Vibrissae (VIH-brih-see) on the chin, nose, arms, and area around the eyes are key to a squirrel's sense of touch. These are similar to whiskers.

ENEMIES & DEFENSES

Squirrels have many predators, and they come from above and below. Hawks, eagles, and owls are among the flying predators that look for a squirrel meal.

Squirrels must be watchful of creatures on the ground as well. Foxes, lynx, weasels, minks, and fishers are just a few of their land-loving predators. Wolves, coyotes, martens, and rattlesnakes are also a threat.

Squirrels use their calls to scare or distract predators. The eastern gray uses high-pitched calls for flying predators. Predators below receive a barking call.

The squirrel's best defense is escape. Thanks to its quick movements, **agility**, and climbing skills, it is often successful. Taken by surprise, the squirrel fights **aggressively** to defend itself.

In addition, a squirrel's fur color helps it stay safe. Lighter belly coloring helps squirrels blend in with the sky when seen from below. From above, a squirrel's darker back helps it blend in with the ground.

Scientists are not sure if a black squirrel's coat color helps or hurts its defense against predators.

THRIVING SPECIES

Escaping the traps and guns of humans is a greater challenge than escaping natural predators. Humans hunt squirrels for their meat and fur and for sport. Squirrel hunting is legal in specific seasons. These differ by state and province.

However, direct contact with squirrels is unwise. Squirrels carry **parasites** on their skin and inside their bodies. They can have mites, chiggers, fleas, ticks, lice, and roundworm. The list goes on. So do not touch squirrels, whether they are dead or alive!

In nature, squirrels provide a valuable service. Their **foraging** and hoarding spreads seeds and mushrooms. This promotes new growth of many types of plants.

Unfortunately, squirrels sometimes do more damage than good. For example, the red squirrel can damage pine trees by eating their bark, cones, and new buds. Eastern gray squirrels feast on fields of corn, wheat, and fruit. Farmers suffer the loss of their valuable crops. Squirrels can also chew through a building's wiring, insulation, and siding.

AT RISK
Habitat loss threatens fox squirrels in some locations.

Still, humans and squirrels share their **habitats** well. Most squirrel species are widespread and thriving. For these reasons, red, fox, and eastern gray squirrels are listed as least concern on the **IUCN Red List**. So, these smart creatures will remain a common and entertaining sight in backyards around North America.

Squirrels that live near humans face additional dangers, such as cars and other threats.

GLOSSARY

aggressive (uh-GREH-sihv) - displaying hostility.

agility - the ability to move quickly and easily.

arboreal (ahr-BAWR-ee-uhl) - living in or frequenting trees.

arid - lacking enough rainfall to support agriculture.

cache (KASH) - a secure or hidden place in which to store something. Something stored in such a place can also be called a cache.

canopy - a protective covering, such as the uppermost spreading, branchy layer of a forest.

deciduous (dih-SIH-juh-wuhs) - shedding leaves each year. Deciduous forests have trees or shrubs that do this.

evolve - to develop gradually.

foraging - searching, especially for food.

habitat - a place where a living thing is naturally found.

hibernate - to spend a period of time, such as the winter, in deep sleep.

IUCN Red List - a list of species that defines how at risk each species is of becoming extinct. The IUCN is the International Union for Conservation of Nature. It is a global environmental organization focused on conservation.

parasite - an organism that lives off of another living thing of a different species.

pregnant - having one or more babies growing within the body.

suburb - a town, village, or community just outside a city.

temperate - having neither very hot nor very cold weather.

tundra - cold, dry, treeless land in the Arctic. Below the surface, the ground is permanently frozen.

urban - of or relating to a city.

WEBSITES

To learn more about Backyard Animals,
visit **booklinks.abdopublishing.com**. These links are routinely
monitored and updated to provide the most current information available.

INDEX